with

ADD/ADHD

(ATTENTION DEFICIT DISORDER/ ATTENTION DEFICIT HYPERACTIVITY DISORDER)

JAYDENE MORRISON, M.S.

The Rosen Publishing Group, Inc.
New York

Published in 1996, 2000 by The Rosen Publishing Group, Inc.
29 East 21st Street, New York, NY 10010

Revised Edition 2000

Library of Congress Cataloging-in-Publication Data

Morrison, Jaydene.
    Coping with ADD/ADHD attention deficit disorder/attention deficit hyperactivity disorder / Jaydene Morrison.
    P.   cm.
    Includes bibliographical references and index.
    Summary: Identifies the syndrome of attention deficit disorder and discusses the appropriate treatment and counseling.
    ISBN 0-8239-3196-X
    1. Attention-deficit hyperactivity disorder-juvenile literature.
[1. Attention-deficit hyperactivity disorder.] I. Title.
RJ506.H9M665 1995
618.92'8589-dc2O
                        95-41284
                           CIP
                           AC

Manufactured in the United States of America

About the Author

Jaydene Morrison is a native-born Oklahoman of pioneer stock. Her great-grandfather was a country doctor who made the historical Cherokee Strip Run into Oklahoma in 1893. Holder of eight teaching certificates, Jaydene is a nationally certified school psychologist, with a master's degree from Oklahoma State University plus more than 60 hours of additional training from OSU and other universities. She is a licensed professional counselor (LPC) and licensed marriage and family therapist (LMFT).

Jaydene's family consists of her two sons, Jay and Mac, and their wives, Kerri and Lori. Blair Morrison is her delightful granddaughter.

Jaydene is presently enjoying the Hawaiian sunsets while working for the Department of Education in Hawaii.

Acknowledgments

It is with deep appreciation that I acknowledge Carla Morrison for her proofreading and valuable suggestions on this book. Carla is a library media specialist at Jarman Junior High School in the Mid-Del public school system.

A special thank-you to my friends, my mother, Katy Walker, and especially my children, Mac, Lori, Jay, and Kerri Morrison, for their support and understanding during the writing of this book.

Contents

Another Bad Day for Suki

Suki Malone was having a bad day. Actually, she seemed to be having a bad day every day, but today was particularly rotten. Both Suki's math teacher and her history teacher had yelled at her in front of the whole class for not paying attention. Her geography teacher had given her another detention for "not settling down"—the third that month. And at lunch, her friend May had told her off for interrupting the conversation so often. "Sometimes you just don't know when to shut up," May had said in an angry tone.

Later on, when Suki's mom got home from work, she was annoyed that Suki hadn't made dinner. "I started to, Mom," explained Suki. "But then May called and after I talked to her, I forgot all about dinner."

"Well, what else is new?" snapped Mrs. Malone. "You never remember to do anything you're supposed to around this place. Honestly! I wonder what goes through that head of yours."

Suki felt really down. Why was everybody always mad at her? Okay, maybe it was true that sometimes she had trouble paying attention in class, that she had a tendency to butt into other people's conversations, and that she got easily distracted and often didn't finish what she had started. But she didn't mean to be such a horrible person. Sometimes she wondered if there was something wrong with "that head" of hers.

The only person who never seemed to get on Suki's case was her English teacher, Ms. Briskie. Her other teachers often complained that Suki was too slow, that she never completed her homework, and that she didn't pay attention to questions. Although Ms. Briskie admitted that Suki needed to focus more, she also frequently praised Suki's rich vocabulary and wonderful imagination.

The day after Suki's really bad day, Suki had to get to school early for her detention. Sitting at her desk with her head down, Suki thought about the day ahead and was suddenly so depressed that she began to cry. Luckily, Ms. Briskie was on detention supervision. She took Suki aside and listened as Suki talked to her about her problems.

"I'm just a big loser," sobbed Suki. "I never do anything right."

"You're not a loser, Suki," said Ms. Briskie. "But it sounds to me as if your problems could be the result of something called ADD."

"ADD?" repeated Suki, looking worried. "Is that a disease?"

"No, Suki," replied Ms. Briskie. "ADD stands for attention deficit disorder. People with ADD have trouble paying attention and can sometimes act impulsively. There's a similar disorder called ADHD—attention deficit hyperactivity disorder— which causes people to behave hyperactively as

well. A medical doctor diagnosed my younger sister with ADHD when she was around your age. That's why I know about it. She was tested at school and then the doctor reviewed her test results and discovered she had ADHD.

"Because it was affecting her ability to learn and do well in school, my sister ended up receiving special help that allowed her to deal with her problems."

"Really?" Suki looked doubtful.

"Yes, really," replied Ms. Briskie. "Listen, Suki, lots of kids your age have ADD or ADHD—between 3 and 5 percent of American kids have one or the other. If it does turn out that you have ADD, know that you're not alone and that there are plenty of ways of overcoming your difficulties."

Later in English class, Ms. Briskie gave Suki a book called A Parent's Guide: Attention Deficit Hyperactivity Disorder in Children by Sam Goldstein. Suki couldn't wait for lunch hour to come so she could begin reading it. Among other things, the book said that kids with ADD/ADHD have difficulty:

↪ Beginning activities

↪ Keeping their attention focused throughout an entire activity

↪ Focusing on more than one thing at a time— such as watching a film and taking notes

↪ Screening out distracting events going on around them

3

⮑ *Thinking before they act*

⮑ *Weighing the consequences of their actions*

⮑ *Planning future actions*

⮑ *Following rules*

The book discussed how people who have diffi-culty paying attention and are easily distracted could experience poor results in many situations, such as in school. It also explored the many problems that could result from impulsive behavior. Suki could sure relate to that. Her parents and friends were always getting annoyed at her for barging into conversations, being tactless, or running ahead and doing something before anyone had asked her to.

"Gee, Ms. Briskie," Suki said when she returned the book to her teacher at the end of the school day. "If I really do have ADD, this book made me feel a whole lot better. I just wish my mom and dad could read this. They think I'm hopeless."

Ms. Briskie not only lent Suki her book, but she drove Suki home from school and together they talked to Mrs. Malone. Ms. Briskie told Mrs. Malone all about ADD and ADHD and all about her sister. She said that she would help conduct the tests that Suki would take at school to see if she had the dis-order. If Suki did have ADD, Ms. Briskie would talk to all the teachers and the principal and make every-one aware of Suki's problems. In spite of Suki's diffi-culties, Ms. Briskie was sure that she and all the other teachers would pitch in to help Suki perform well in school.

After Ms. Briskie left the house, Suki noticed that her mom was looking sad and serious. She was expecting her mom to yell at her for being a mess-up. Instead, Mrs. Malone gave her a huge hug.

"Oh, Suki," said her mom. "I'm so sorry I was always on your case for being late and careless and irresponsible and goofing off. I really had no idea that your behavior and your poor grades could have been due to a disorder. If it turns out that you really do have this ADD—or anything else—your dad and I are going to be with you every step of the way, kiddo. Just like that Ms. Briskie."

That night when Suki went to sleep, she found herself feeling happy for the first time in ages. She realized that today had been the first time in a long time that she hadn't had a bad day. And if Ms. Briskie was right, her bad days might be coming to an end—for good.

What Is
ADD/ADHD?

Based on current research, most experts believe that ADD/ADHD is a neurobiological disorder. "Neurobiological" refers to the structure, chemistry, and function of parts of the brain. In people with ADD/ADHD, there may be imbalances or differences in the chemicals used by the brain to control activity, attention, motor skills, and some other aspects of behavior. A recent study published in the *Archives of General Psychiatry* found that while the right side of the "normal" human brain is usually larger than the left side, in people with ADD/ADHD both sides tend to be abnormally similar in size.

What could cause these differences? No single cause is known. Heredity seems to play a strong role. If you have ADD/ADHD, you may have inherited it from a parent. Problems during pregnancy or at birth may also play a part. ADD/ADHD has nothing to do with intelligence. And most specialists see no link with sugar, food additives, or inner-ear problems, all of which have been studied for possible connections. ADD/ADHD is a recognized diagnosis, both medically and legally. However, some doctors, psychologists, and others continue to debate whether it really is a disorder in its own right or a convenient way to describe a number of symptoms or problems. Researchers continue to look for definitive answers.

A Deficit in Attention

Everyone has trouble focusing attention sometimes. There can be many reasons you can't concentrate and listen. Perhaps you're upset about a relationship with someone. Or you're mad at your parents. Or you have exciting plans coming up and they're all you can think about. These distractions are temporary. Soon you find you can pay attention again.

But some people have had attention problems for as long as they can remember. They can seldom concentrate on the subject at hand for more than a few minutes. This can sometimes be a symptom of ADD.

Other people have long-term attention problems and are also hyperactive. This means they are too active. They can't sit still and are always moving and fidgeting. These can be symptoms of attention deficit hyperactivity disorder, or ADHD.

As many as 3 to 5 percent of school-age children may have ADD/ADHD. Both boys and girls are affected, but the diagnosis is made more often in boys. This could be in part because boys have hyperactivity symptoms more than girls do, which makes the symptoms more noticeable. Adults may think a teenager who has ADD symptoms without hyperactivity is unmotivated or depressed, and they may fail to notice the attention-related problems.

Overdiagnosis

Although ADD/ADHD may not be recognized often enough in some cases, many doctors worry that it is

7

inaccurately diagnosed much too often in young people. These children and teens are being incorrectly treated and medicated, and frequently the real causes of their problems go unsolved.

Why is there overdiagnosis? Probably several factors combine to produce these mistakes. First, ADD/ADHD can be difficult to diagnose. There is no laboratory test for it, as the American Psychiatric Association's *Diagnostic and Statistical Manual of Mental Disorders* points out. It is not diagnosed by its cause, which is unknown, but by descriptions and evaluations of its symptoms. These are often the same as symptoms of other disorders, such as depression or anxiety. Doctors must rule out all the other possibilities before diagnosing ADD/ADHD.

Parents and teachers may be overeager for a diagnosis of ADD/ADHD, especially if children or teens have behavior problems that the adults are anxious to get under control. Everyone wants to come up with an answer, and they may be too quick to hit upon ADD/ADHD. They may even try to fit the teen's symptoms into the ADD/ADHD pattern when they don't really fit.

It won't help you with your problems to be treated for ADD/ADHD if you don't have it. If you are being tested, try to talk frankly to your doctor, your parents, and the evaluation team throughout the diagnostic process.

ADD/ADHD must be carefully diagnosed because many other problems, such as depression or learning disabilities, have similar symptoms. Thorough testing and evaluation may reveal a learning disability, a serious emotional disturbance, a hearing problem, or a speech or language difficulty. It is possible to have any of these difficulties and to have ADD/ADHD also. So how do you know if you have ADD/ADHD?

As a result, ADD/ADHD may even be underdiagnosed for many teens. Their problems may be missed altogether or be mistakenly attributed to other causes.

Symptoms

To diagnose ADD/ADHD, a health care professional requires information about you and your symptoms from a variety of sources. To identify symptoms, doctors refer to the American Psychiatric Association's *Diagnostic and Statistical Manual of Mental Disorders (DSM-IV)*, fourth edition—the authority in defining mental health and developmental health difficulties.

As you will see from the following lists, which are summarized from the DSM-IV, ADD and ADHD symptoms are related but not exactly the same. For ADD or ADHD to be diagnosed, some problems with attention or impulsiveness must have started before the age of seven, even if they were not diagnosed then. The symptoms must have existed for more than six months, and they must affect you in at least two settings, such as home and school. They must interfere with how you should be functioning at your age, for example, with your schoolwork. And they must not be the direct result of another problem, such as an anxiety disorder, although you may have other such problems.

ADD Symptoms

⮑ Difficulty paying attention

9

- Difficulty sustaining attention

- Difficulty listening

- Difficulty completing tasks

- Difficulty with organizational skills

- Avoiding tasks requiring sustained effort

- Losing things

- Easily distracted

- Forgetting things

ADHD Symptoms

- Fidgeting and squirming

- Leaving seat often

- Difficulty with quiet leisure activities

- Being always on the go

- Talking excessively

- Blurting out answers

- Difficulty waiting turns

- Interrupting or intruding on others

- Running or climbing excessively (in teenagers or adults, extreme restlessness)

Evaluation

Not everyone fits neatly into one category or the other—
ADD or ADHD. It is possible that you may have symptoms of both at times.

If you have six or more of these symptoms for more than
six months, a thorough assessment should be made to
determine if you have ADD or ADHD. The following for-
mat is a common one for a health care professional to use
for an evaluation:

- Parent interview

- Teacher interview

- Observation in classroom

- Student (child or teen) interview

- Behavior rating scales (completed by teacher and
  parents)

- Medical evaluation

- Testing (intellectual, achievement, and fine-motor
  skills)

Many experts have published rating scales. Ask your librar-
ian to show you where they are kept.

Parents have a wealth of information about their children. They can tell the interviewer about the child's or
teen's current symptoms and behavior. The interviewer
will also want to know about the early development of the
child, such as walking and talking. The parents will be

asked if the young child listened, was impulsive, or was more active than other children. This kind of information is important in diagnosing ADD/ADHD.

Teachers are also a valuable source of information. They know how a student's attention span and activity levels compare to those of others students of that age. In addition, someone other than the teacher should observe the student in the classroom for more insight.

The interviewer will also speak to the teen or child to hear his description of the problems he is encountering and anything else he would like to discuss.

Parents and teachers fill out written questionnaires. These behavior rating scales are lists of questions about how the child responds to certain activities and tasks. For example, a common question on the parents' list is "Do you consider your child to be more active than most children his age?"

The student is often asked to take several tests. Some tests can help screen out or identify learning disabilities and other problems, both psychological and physical.

Intelligence tests help an evaluator to assess the student's level of ability. People with ADD/ADHD can have intelligence of any level—high, average, or low. For many years, people thought a person's intelligence was set in stone. We have now learned that ability level or intellectual level can be changed. Experiences and environment play a role in ability or intellectual level.

Achievement tests show the grade level at which the student is working. For example, a student can be working at a ninth-grade level in math and a second-grade level in reading.

Fine-motor tests may consist of paper-and-pencil activities and other tests of the student's finger coordination and speed. Students with fine-motor difficulties are slow in completing their written work in the classroom. Handwriting is often poor in students with ADD/ADHD.

Finally, the teen or child should have a medical exam by a doctor who is experienced with ADD/ADHD.

All of the information gathered through this process makes possible a complete view of the teen or child. It is rather like looking at different parts of the person under a microscope and then putting all the pieces together to see the whole picture and make the diagnosis.

It can be a great relief to both the teen and the parents to find out that the teen does have ADD/ADHD. At last they all know that the problems are no one's fault. ADD/ADHD is a neurobiological disorder. Now that they know what the problem is, they can start to improve the situation.

Brenda

It seemed as if Brenda could never sit still for more than a few minutes without growing restless. Her mother said she was "fidgety" and her dad said she had "too many ants in her pants." But when she was at home or hanging out with her friends, even though she "acted up" at times, life seemed a lot less complicated.

At school, however, everything was a lot worse. Brenda felt that her teachers were always picking on her. They said she talked too much and couldn't behave herself. And Brenda dreaded the end of each term when she brought home report cards with comments such as "no attention span," "never listens in class," "lacks discipline," and "no motivation." It wasn't true that she lacked motivation, thought Brenda to herself. She wanted to do well. But as the years passed, she seemed to have more and more difficulty paying attention, reading longer books, writing longer essays, and concentrating on exams.

Finally, the guidance counselor at Brenda's school took a look at her records and recommended that she be tested for ADHD. He had the school psychologist interview not only Brenda and her parents, but Brenda's teachers as well. While her parents and teachers filled out some questionnaires rating Brenda's behavior, Brenda herself was given some tests that required her to read and answer questions. As usual, after some time, Brenda felt fidgety and distracted and then she couldn't concentrate anymore. Although she didn't say anything, the psychologist seemed to know something was the matter and he asked her what was wrong. He told Brenda to relax and take a ten-minute break before continuing the tests. The break seemed to help.

Based on the interviews, the ratings, and Brenda's test results, Brenda's doctor wrote an official diagnosis of attention deficit hyperactivity disorder, or ADHD. The doctor also prescribed some medication to help reduce Brenda's symptoms. At first Brenda was to take only small doses in order to measure carefully her reactions to the medication. Meanwhile, back at school, Brenda and her parents met with the psychologist again to go over some *techniques that would help Brenda deal with her disorder and perform better at school. They also met with her teachers and her guidance counselor to develop a plan that would take Brenda's special needs into consideration while letting her keep up with the rest of the class. Brenda hoped that the medication she was taking and the new techniques she was learning would help her be able to concentrate and stop fidgeting.*

Medication to Help Manage ADD/ADHD

If you have been diagnosed with ADD/ADHD, your doctor will probably suggest that you try one or more of the medications commonly used to treat attention deficit disorders. Medication will not cure ADD/ADHD, and it will not control your behavior. What medication can do is help improve your symptoms. An improvement in your symptoms, such as lengthening your attention span, will make it easier for you to work on the ADD/ADHD-related problems you encounter at school, at home, and with your friends.

Medication, if used, will be only one part of the treatment of your ADD/ADHD. Complete treatment of attention deficit disorders must be multimodal. This means that they must be treated by several methods at the same time. A multimodal treatment plan might include medication, therapy or counseling for you and your family, behavior management, and a school plan. Other parts of the multimodal plan are discussed further in chapter 4.

Medication can be helpful for about three quarters of children with ADD/ADHD. Others may experience side effects or find that medication doesn't improve their symptoms. Your doctor may want you to try several different medications to find the best one for you.

The dosage needed varies from person to person. Your doctor will prescribe a certain dosage to start. Then you, your parents, and your teachers will observe your behavior for several days. The dosage will be adjusted until you reach the best level.

You and your parents should learn about ADD/ADHD medications before deciding whether you should try them. If you do decide to try medication, it is important to pay attention to how it is affecting you. Each person's body reacts differently to various drugs. The appendix of this book has a fact sheet published by CH.A.D.D. (Children and Adults with Attention Deficit Disorder) about medications and their effects. In addition, the following monitoring chart can help you keep track of the doses of each drug you take and monitor any side effects. You should also ask your doctor to discuss with you and your parents how often you should take your medication. You may find it best to maintain the same level of medication in all situations year-round. Some teens do better varying their medication, depending on whether they're at home, at school, or on vacation. You should not make any changes in your prescribed course of medication without talking to your doctor first.

The drugs used to treat ADD/ADHD are not addictive. But they can have side effects for some people, and, in a small percentage of people, serious effects such as Tourette's syndrome, which is a neurological disorder involving involuntary movements and behavior. That is why it is important to pay attention to how any medication affects you.

Medication Monitoring Charts

The person being treated, the parents, and teachers should all fill out charts like these because the teen's reactions and behavior may vary throughout the day. Give the completed charts to the doctor who prescribed the medication at your next visit. He or she will use the information to adjust the dosage and type of medication.

MEDICATIONS DOSAGE
(List all medications below)

Name: Date:
Birth date: Age: Grade:

Medication	Dose	Frequency	Time Taken

Variations in frequency or other comments:

REACTIONS AND BEHAVIOR
(Note all reactions and behavior below)

Day:
Date:
Time:
Place observed:
Name of person filling out chart:

Social Behaviors	Better	Worse	No Change	Comments
Peer Interaction				
Parent Interaction				
Teacher Interaction				
Task-Related				
Listening				
Inattention				
Impatience				

18

Social Behaviors	Better	Worse	No Change	Comments
Distractibility				
Completing Work				
Handling Interruptions				
Physical/Emotional				
Fidgety				
Impulsiveness				
Activity Level				
Moody				
Bored				
Difficulty with				
Rules/Authority				

SIDE EFFECTS
(Note all side effects experienced)

Day:
Date:
Time:
Place observed:
Name of person filling out chart:

Social Behaviors	Better	Worse	No Change	Comments
Nervousness				
Sleeplessness				
Vomiting				
Skin Rash				
Dizziness				
Headaches				
Depression				
Loss of Appetite				
Irritability				
Confusion				
Stomachaches				
Excessive Crying				
Motor/Vocal Tic				
Other (describe)				

Overmedication

There are other reasons to be cautious about using medication. As we saw in chapter 2, ADD/ADHD may be incorrectly diagnosed in many young people. This means that they may take medication for a condition they don't have. This is not a good idea. In other cases, some young people who do have a disorder could have first tried to treat it without medication. Their doctors may have been too quick to prescribe medication, especially if their parents and teachers were desperate to see an improvement in behavior. Finally, it is important that the doctor determine the minimum dosage needed. Taking more medication than you need can affect you negatively.

You may hate the idea of using any drugs, or you may be embarrassed about taking them, especially at school. Your parents may have negative feelings about letting you take medication and be concerned about the effect on your overall health. Your concerns and worries are very important. You and your parents should carefully discuss the pros and cons of the ADD/ADHD medications with your doctor and the other people who have been involved in the diagnosis.

Write a list of questions that you and your parents want to ask your doctor. Take it to your appointment so you won't forget to ask anything. Write down the answers too. Don't be afraid to ask the doctor to explain anything you don't understand. ADD/ADHD is a complicated topic, and the answers are very important—more important to you than to anyone else. Here are some questions to start your list.

1. What are the possible short-term negative effects of the medication?

2. What are the possible long-term negative effects?

3. How will we find the lowest possible dosage I can take?

4. How would this drug interact with other substances I might take, such as cold medicines and caffeine?

5. Should I take the medication all the time, or just on school days?

6. Do I need to get the medication in the middle of the day at school from the school nurse?

7. What happens if I forget to take my medication? Should I take my next dose at the regular time?

8. How often will we evaluate my continuing to use the drugs?

9. When can I or my parents call you if we have new questions about the medication?

10. How can I find out about the costs of the drugs and whether our insurance plan will cover them?

If you or your parents feel that your doctor is urging the use of medication too quickly, when non medical methods could be tried first, or if you or your parents have any lingering doubts after speaking with your doctor, you can always seek a second medical opinion.

You can get more information about ADD/ADHD medications from the support groups listed in the Where to Go for Help section in this book and from some of the books listed in the For Further Reading section. The more you educate yourself about ADD/ADHD, the more carefully you can decide whether or not to try medication.

Stimulants

Stimulant medications are most often prescribed for ADD/ADHD. For people without ADD/ADHD, a stimulant drug increases activity. For those with attention deficit disorders, however, stimulants have a very different effect. Their general positive effects can include:

- Increased visual-motor coordination

- Less oppositional behavior

- Decreased aggressiveness

- Decreased talkativeness

- More task-oriented behavior.

General possible side effects (short-term or long-term) of stimulants can include:

- Reduced appetite

22

⇝ Sleep problems

⇝ Weight and growth pattern suppression

⇝ Nausea, headaches, dizziness, abdominal discomfort

⇝ Motor or vocal tics, such as Tourette's syndrome, especially if there is a family history of tics

Stimulant Medications for ADD/ADHD

Ritalin *(generic name: methylphenidate)*
Ritalin is the most commonly prescribed drug for ADD/ADHD. Its effects can be seen within thirty to ninety minutes after being taken orally. Ritalin is available in tablet form in doses of 5 milligrams (mg), 10 mg, 20 mg, and sustained release SR 20 mg.

Dexedrine *(generic name: dextroamphetamine)*
Some people with ADD/ADHD do better with Dexedrine than with Ritalin. This drug is available in 5-mg tablets, as well as in time-released capsules. The user generally can notice the effects within thirty to ninety minutes.

Cylert *(generic name: pemoline)*
Cylert is slower acting but longer lasting than Ritalin or Dexedrine. Cylert may take three to six weeks to reach maximum effectiveness. Liver function tests are recommended prior to and periodically during use.

Nonstimulant Medications for ADD/ADHD

Catapres *(generic name: clonidine)*
Catapres is an antihypertensive drug that has recently been used for some hyperactive persons, but not for those who have ADD without hyperactivity. It is available in tablets or as a patch worn on the skin like a Band-Aid. The effects are seen within an hour. Nausea, rashes, drowsiness, dryness of the nose and mouth, Tourette's Syndrome, constipation, and light-headedness are some of the possible side effects.

Tofranil *(generic name: imipramine) and* **Norpramin** *(generic name: desipramine)*
Sometimes people with ADD/ADHD are depressed or feel too many side effects from the stimulants they are taking. They may be given antidepressants, such as Tofranil or Norpramin. These drugs can also be helpful in reducing hyperactivity and aggression. Side effects can include sensitivity to sunlight, tiredness, mild stomach disturbances, and sleep disorders. These drugs can affect the user's heart rate, so the doctor must monitor the heart carefully.

Alfonso

As usual, Alfonso got into a big fight with his mother right before they were about to leave for the doctor's office. His mother yelled at him for having forgotten about the appointment, for not being ready on time, and for being dressed like a slob. Alfonso yelled back that he didn't want to go to a doctor and that she could go by herself. Finally, after a lot more yelling, mother and son left, arriving at Dr. McGraw's office over an hour late.

Four months before—after years of getting into plenty of fights and trouble at school—Alfonso had been diagnosed with ADHD. Since then, he had been working with the school psychologist to try to control his aggressive and impulsive behavior. The techniques he had been learning were helping somewhat, but he still had trouble keeping his temper and staying out of trouble with other kids. The previous week, he had been suspended for punching out Billy Sucrière. Afterward, the psychologist told Alfonso's mother that Alfonso might need more than just counseling to deal with his ADHD—he might need to go on medication.

When his mother told him this, Alfonso hit the roof. "I don't want to be a junkie dependent on popping pills! All the other kids will think I'm mental!" he yelled. He listened to Dr. McGraw talk about how his medical history made him a good candidate for a non addictive drug called Ritalin. Alfonso thought it might be worth a try, especially since Dr. McGraw said that taking Ritalin would help calm Alfonso's anger and ease his restlessness. It would also allow him to concentrate better on activities such as reading, writing, and listening to others.

Already at the end of his first week of taking Ritalin, Alfonso felt that the medication was making a difference. The only problem was that he was experiencing some mild headaches and a bit of nausea.

When, at the end of the week, Alfonso went back to the doctor for a check up, Dr. McGraw decreased the dosage slightly so that the negative side effects would disappear. A few days later, they had. And Alfonso decided to keep using Ritalin, all the while continuing with his therapy and behavior management.

Within a few months, Alfonso realized that he was actually getting most of his homework done and was able to do better on tests and quizzes. His grades had improved quite a bit and he rarely got yelled at anymore. For the first time in ages, he realized that he was actually liking school. Not only was he getting along with his teachers, but he was also getting along with the other kids who used to think he was a big mouth and a bully. Instead of feeling angry and frustrated with himself, he started thinking he was a pretty good guy after all. And although the Ritalin was a great help, he took pride in the fact that a lot of his success in overcoming his problems was due to his taking charge of his behavior.

Alternatives to Medication

Although medication can be of great help to many teens with ADD/ADHD, not everyone benefits from medication and not everyone wants to use it. Researchers continue to look for ways to improve ADD/ADHD symptoms without medication. For example, some people are using EEG biofeedback (electroencephalogram). This is a method of measuring certain activity in parts of the brain and then training the person to alter his brain wave activity to improve attention span and decrease hyperactivity.

Other people have studied the treatment of ADD/ADHD through the control of diet. Some treatments eliminate substances such as sugar and food additives. Others focus on increasing the intake of certain vitamins and minerals. To date, these studies have not provided evidence of effectiveness that is accepted by most mainstream experts. Some alternative treatments are considered very controversial and others are considered to be worth more research. Some appear to be useful for small numbers of people with ADD/ADHD.

For teens with ADD/ADHD and their parents, it can be very tempting to try the latest experimental treatment, especially when someone else says that it helped them. It is wise to proceed cautiously, to read all the available information pro and con, and to discuss all possible treatments with trusted health care professionals.

Whether or not you use medication in the treatment of your ADD/ADHD, you will certainly need to use several other methods of management, as we shall see in the following chapter.

Techniques to Help Manage ADD/ADHD

A multimodal treatment of ADD/ADHD is extremely important to ensure your success. This means using many methods at the same time. You cannot rely only on medication. Multimodal treatments may include:

⮌ Behavior management techniques

⮌ Organizational techniques

⮌ An educational plan for you to use in school and for homework

⮌ Counseling or therapy for you or your parents or both

⮌ Medication

Multimodal treatment requires the cooperation of you, your parents, your teachers and school staff, your doctor, and your counselor or therapist. ADD/ADHD is not a problem that you have just at home or at school. It affects you in many areas and in many ways, and it must be treated as such for you to get the best possible results.

Behavior Management Techniques

Once you have been diagnosed with ADD/ADHD, your counselor, therapist, or other professional trained in ADD/ADHD can help you and your parents develop a behavior management plan. This might include:

- Identifying the specific behavior you need to change

- Setting up a structured system of immediate rewards and penalties for each time you show a particular appropriate or inappropriate behavior

- Making a specific plan on how to avoid unconstructive arguments and fights and to manage your anger

Organizational Techniques

Teens with ADD/ADHD are frequently disorganized. You may lose things, forget dates, and do incomplete homework. Your counselor can help you develop methods to keep track of important information and tasks by using simple tools such as special notebooks, color-coded files, and timers. These can be a big help in compensating for some of your symptoms and improving your performance in school.

Educational Plan

Students with ADD/ADHD usually need some classroom changes in order to perform at their best. These changes can range from sitting up front in the classroom to special structures for taking tests or extra help from the teacher. Students who also have learning disabilities may need special education classes.

Two federal laws pertain to the educational needs of students with ADD/ADHD. One is the Individuals with Disabilities Education Act (IDEA); the other is Section 504 of the Rehabilitation Act of 1973. Because many schools do not realize that ADD/ADHD is a disability, the U.S. Department of Education issued a "Policy Clarification Memorandum" in 1991 to make it clear that ADD/ADHD qualifies students for reasonable accommodations if their disorder severely affects their performance in school.

Whether a student qualifies for this help is determined by a complete evaluation of the student's school experience. Your parents should write a letter requesting that the school do an evaluation to see if you can receive educational help under these laws.

If you do qualify, you and your parents and school will create a 504 Plan to meet your particular learning needs. Your educational plan can be one of your most useful tools to cope with ADD/ADHD in school. It is important that you get all the help to which you are legally entitled in order to develop your plan and put it into practice. Your educational rights are discussed in chapter 5.

Counseling and Therapy

Therapy may be recommended by your doctor. Therapy can be useful to a teen with ADD/ADHD who is also experiencing depression, low self-esteem, or other psychological problems. Your parents may also benefit from therapy to discuss all the stresses and strains that coping with ADD/ADHD puts on them.

A counselor trained in ADD/ADHD is another person who can help. A counselor can help you create and follow treatment plans like the ones discussed earlier. You can learn about proven treatment plans and tailor them to your individual needs by working with a professional counselor.

Support Groups

You and your parents should also find out about local support groups for parents and children coping with ADD/ADHD. Call or write the national organizations listed in the Where to Go for Help section at the end of this book. They will send you information about membership fees and what local chapters are located near you. One national group is CH.A.D.D., or Children and Adults with Attention Deficit Disorder. CH.A.D.D. has more than 20,000 members and 500 local chapters nationwide. It publishes very useful fact sheets about different aspects of ADD/ADHD.

Educating yourself about your disorder is one of the best ways you can learn to manage it. The support groups can help you stay up-to-date on the latest research. Most people also find it helpful to talk to others who have similar problems, and you may find that you enjoy meeting other people with ADD/ADHD.

Valerie

When Valerie was first diagnosed with ADD, she

learned from her doctor that aside from going to counseling and learning behavior management, she might want to try taking medication. When she heard this, Valerie was upset. She didn't like the idea of taking drugs; she hated swallowing pills and didn't want to have the responsibility of remembering to take them. She had a long talk with her parents, who said they would be behind her 100 percent in helping her organize her schedule and get her schoolwork and studying done without having to resort to medication.

Valerie's mother found a specialized therapist who had experience creating behavior management programs for young people with ADD. Valerie, her parents, and the therapist identified Valerie's biggest problems—forgetting to take her assignments home, not completing her homework, and being unable to study for long periods of time. They then developed an organization plan for Valerie to follow, one that her parents and teachers would help her maintain.

Valerie bought a time management planner with dates on every page, and lots of room to write on. She carried it around with her to all of her classes. Each time her teachers announced an assignment, an essay, or a test, Valerie made sure she wrote down all the information on the necessary page. Before leaving class, she always asked her teacher to initial the annotation. This way both she and her teacher knew that Valerie had all the correct information. At the end of each day, Valerie scanned her agenda and made sure she took home all the books she needed for any test or homework assignment.

At home, Valerie's parents looked at her agenda and always knew what work she needed to complete. Sometimes, they had to nudge her a bit, when Valerie was feeling restless or antsy. They let Valerie take breaks from reading or studying, but they let her know that if she did not finish something, she would not be able to go out with her friends on the weekend. If she did finish everything, then she could. This system of rewards and punishments helped keep Valerie motivated, especially on the days when she really didn't feel like doing any work or when she had trouble getting herself motivated.

Sometimes, Valerie felt as if she were a prisoner, with no control over her own life. She had to make sure that her teachers initialed all of her assignments and that her parents verified that she did everything she was supposed to do. At the same time, she had to keep seeing her therapist every week in order to deal with some of the problematic ADD symptoms that affected not only her academic life, but her home life and social life as well.

Little by little, however, she realized that it wasn't that everybody else was controlling her life, but that she, herself, was. She was increasingly able to finish her assignments and went into tests feeling that she had studied well. Her grades started to improve. And also, her relationships with her family and friends were going much more smoothly than they ever had before.

Valerie began feeling really good about herself. She had turned her life around. And she had done it the way she wanted to—without taking medication.

Joey

Joey was doing research at the library. He had to write a paper about ADD/ADHD. It wasn't his idea; one of his teachers had assigned him the topic. As he looked through the books and articles on ADD/ADHD, Joey felt he was reading about himself. He knew that he had a short attention span and that it had always been hard for him to sit still. He was always fidgeting in his seat and getting things in and out of his desk. It wasn't that he was trying to create problems. Sometimes he just wondered where he had put something and decided to look in his desk for it. School was boring anyway. Sometimes things his teachers mentioned reminded him of something else. When the teacher accused him of not listening, it seemed to Joey that he had been listening.

One book he read said that distractibility was a symptom of ADD/ADHD. Yes, Joey felt that he had a distractibility problem, too. If the student next to him began tapping his pencil, Joey couldn't hear the teacher. All he could hear was the pencil tapping. Sometimes he heard the teacher talking in the class-room next door instead of his own teacher. The school had checked his hearing several times. Maybe it wasn't his hearing. Maybe it was distractibility.

The subject of medication caught Joey's attention. "It would be great if I could take a pill and change everything," he thought. As Joey read on, he found that medication was helpful for many teens with ADD/ADHD, but not all. He decided to ask his doctor about it.

Next Joey read about losing track of time. He knew he often tried to do too many things in one day instead of focusing on the important ones. He copied the Time-Monitoring Chart to help him see how he used his time every day.

Joey kept reading. He found some behavior management techniques for ADD/ADHD called cognitive control strategies. He thought maybe he could try them himself and see if they worked. He started to take notes:

1. Monitor myself during class or when reading by making tally marks on a piece of paper whenever I drift from material.

2. Take notes in class or from the book. Have the teacher check to see if I wrote down the most important things.

3. To remember things better, make mental pictures. Repeat things over and over. Make associations by thinking of things the subject reminds me of. Make acronyms out of the first letters of words to make remembering easier.

4. Make note cards or lists and highlight important information.

5. Make maps or diagrams in order to see how ideas are connected.

6. Develop a study schedule. Make a chart to keep track of time to study each subject.

TIME-MONITORING CHART

On a typical busy day, keep a Time-Monitoring Chart. Write down all the things you do.

Activity	Time	Purpose of Activity	Results	Emotional Feeling About Activity
___	___	___	___	___
___	___	___	___	___
___	___	___	___	___
___	___	___	___	___

1. What did you accomplish? _____
_____

2. How many activities did you enjoy? _____
_____

3. Were you happy or unhappy? (State what made the difference) _____
_____

4. Now plan how to change the ways you use your time.
_____

(Your parents or counselor can help you.)

7. Ask a counselor or teacher to help me with a study guide and decide on learning strategies to study things.

The books and articles Joey read suggested that the way you dealt with ADD/ADHD could help you be successful. That was interesting. Joey thought that no one is perfect in life. Everyone has some problem to tackle. Maybe his problems were related to ADD/ADHD. He decided to show his parents the research he had done and ask for an appointment with their family doctor.

Making School
Better

Most ADD/ADHD teenagers have felt rejected and disappointed in school. School is a real drag for them a lot of the time.

Schools are often rigid and structured places where students have to sit quietly in one place for long periods. An ADHD teen finds it difficult to sit quietly and consequently is often in conflict with the adults who are trying to enforce the rules. ADD/ADHD students have trouble concentrating and paying attention. They tend to miss a lot in class, including homework assignments. Some students even convince themselves that the teacher never gave the assignment. Often, they really didn't hear what the teacher said. That's the nature of ADD/ADHD.

Legal Rights and Realities

Schools are required by law to accommodate the needs of students with ADD/ADHD who meet certain criteria. Under the Individuals with Disabilities Education Act, students with ADD/ADHD may qualify for reasonable accommodations to meet the student's personalized needs. Under the other law, Section 504 of the Rehabilitation Act of 1973, ADD/ADHD students may qualify to have accommodations made for them within their regular classrooms.

This is the way the system works when everything goes right: Your teachers or your parents think that your problem may be caused by ADD/ADHD and that it is having a major impact on your schooling. Your parents make a written request to the school to have you evaluated and diagnosed. The school has a team of people carry out the required tests, at no cost to your family. Most schools require a medical diagnosis. If you are diagnosed with ADD/ADHD and if the evaluation shows that it significantly affects your school performance, you, your parents, and the people designated by the school write a special plan for your needs in school. For instance, if you need reasonable accommodations, these will be specified. Or if you need changes in your regular classroom, such as extra time to take tests, this will be written in your plan. Then you and your teachers and everyone involved will follow the plan to improve your ability to learn and to do your work. At the same time, you will use other treatment methods for your ADD/ADHD, such as behavior management techniques.

In many schools, students get help quickly and find the staff wonderfully supportive and eager to improve the situation. But in other schools, reality may be quite different. If your school is understaffed, underfunded, and overly crowded, it may be inefficient giving you the help you're entitled to receive. The teachers may be responsible for so many students that they just don't have enough time to give everyone individual attention. Or the people in your school may not understand ADD/ADHD or their legal obligation to help you. And in any school there may be people who just don't care enough to do what they are supposed to do.

Some parents decide to have the evaluation and diagnosis done by professionals who are not connected with the school. Then they must pay the fees themselves. If you and your parents choose this route, you will still need your school to accept the evaluation and diagnosis and to make the changes you need.

Getting your school's cooperation may take persistence, letters, and phone calls. It may require educating the school staff if they are open to receiving information about ADD/ADHD. It could even require taking legal action against the school. If your school is not cooperating, contact one of the ADD/ADHD support groups listed in the back of this book. Through them you can find out more about obtaining your legal rights and how other parents and students got their schools to work with them.

If they are not familiar with current information on ADD/ADHD, teachers and administrators should be given a fact sheet explaining these disorders. CH.A.D.D. (Children and Adults with Attention Deficit Disorder), a national support group, has published an excellent article that is short, to the point, and updated regularly. It is reprinted in the appendix. You can also call or write CH.A.D.D. and ask about its fact sheets for teachers and about your educational rights. You may also want to show your teachers a copy of this book.

Casey

Casey's father was in the military service. Her family moved from place to place as her father was restationed in different parts of the United States and in

40

other countries. It is hard on kids to start at new schools all the time. It was especially hard for Casey because she had ADD and a learning disability. Every time she changed schools, she had to explain herself all over again to new people, and she had to learn a new routine.

Casey had learned from experience to take the initiative herself when she enrolled in a new school. She went directly to the assistant principal or school counselor and gave them a packet that contained the following items:

1. *Letter from a medical doctor with her diagnosis of ADD and her medication requirements. Casey needed to take medication at school in the middle of the day.*

2. *Test results, which included the best learning approach for Casey.*

3. *Individualized Education Plan (IEP) from her previous school.*

4. *Letter from a past teacher explaining what worked best in the classroom.*

5. *Article from Children and Adults with Attention Deficit Disorder (CH.A.D.D.), giving a brief description of ADD/ADHD.*

Casey found that the people in some schools were ready to work with her. In other schools, they did not

41

understand or were not helpful, and she had to try much harder to get their cooperation. Before she entered the classroom, she requested a conference with the principal or assistant principal, the counselor, teachers, her parents, and herself. Casey preferred to take the initiative and do this herself. Casey had a friend named Tawanda who had ADD/ADHD and who had also changed schools a lot. Tawanda always had her parents make the request because she thought the authorities paid more attention to her parents, and it made things easier. Each girl found the best approach for her own situation.

Casey explained her specific problems in the conference and talked about her best learning style, which was a visual approach to learning. She explained that she had poor listening skills and found it hard to remember facts. She did better if she could see the material on overhead projectors, visual aids, or the blackboard. This information was also in her IEP.

In addition to explaining the support she needed, Casey asked what was expected of her. She tried to be reasonable. She realized that teachers have a lot of students to consider. She tried to be assertive about her needs, but never aggressive or rude.

After talking to everyone she would work with, Casey started school. She used some of the organizing and listening techniques her original counselor had worked out with her. At her new school, she was glad to find that she would be in the same classes as Carlos, a student her age who had ADHD. Casey and Carlos soon became good friends. Sharing experiences with each other made them feel less alone.

Carlos

Mr. Jordan was trying to ignore Carlos. He could hear the boy tapping his pencil, shuffling papers on his desk, and whispering to the girl next to him. It seemed to Mr. Jordan that Carlos was purposely trying to irritate him. When Carlos's book crashed loudly to the floor, Mr. Jordan exploded. "Carlos, take your things and go to the office to work. You obviously can't work in here."

The room grew quiet. Carlos felt himself growing numb. When he got into trouble he always went numb so he didn't feel so hurt. As Carlos picked up his things, his pencil and notebook fell to the floor. He nervously picked them up. Everyone was watching. Mr. Jordan just stood and waited, looking angry. Carlos was afraid to ask what the assignment was going to be. He knew he wouldn't be able to do it anyway without hearing Mr. Jordan explain it in class. And then he would be in trouble again when he showed up without the assignment. Carlos was devastated.

It seemed to Carlos as if nothing worked out at school, no matter how hard he tried to manage his ADHD. As he trudged down the hall to the office, he met Ms. Washington, the school counselor. She said, "Carlos, you certainly look down today."

Before he knew it, he had told her the whole story. She went to the office with him and helped him get started on another assignment. Before she left, she assured him that she would help him get things worked out. Later on that day she found Carlos and took him to Mr. Jordan's room. Carlos

43

had trouble looking Mr. Jordan in the eye. Ms. Washington said she and Mr. Jordan had been talking. She asked Carlos to explain what he had been trying to do to cope with his ADHD. She helped him and Mr. Jordan draw up some guidelines that could work for both of them. The guidelines they agreed upon were these:

1. *Carlos would try to be the very first one in the room and to get his materials organized before class began.*

2. *Carlos would write down the assignments.*

3. *Carlos would take notes during the class period. (Writing was difficult for Carlos, so he knew his notes would be brief. If note taking became a distraction for him, he would tell Mr. Jordan, and it could be discontinued.)*

4. *Carlos would raise his hand or hold his pencil up when he needed help or to ask a question.*

5. *Mr. Jordan would walk by and pause beside Carlos's desk twice during each class period to remind him to concentrate. He wouldn't say anything to draw attention to Carlos.*

6. *Mr. Jordan would remember to compliment Carlos privately when he did appropriate things.*

7. *From time to time Carlos and Mr. Jordan would*

discuss whether the guidelines were working or if they should adjust them.

Carlos saw Ms. Washington in the hall a few days later. She took one look at him and said, "Hey, I like

_____'s Homework Assignment

Week: Day: Date:

	English	Math	Science	Social Studies	Other Subject
I listened to the teacher in class (Yes/Some/No)					
Assignment					
Time estimated to do homework					
Homework completed?					
Proofread for errors?					
I took the time for my writing to be neat (Yes/Some/No)					

that big smile on your face these days." Carlos laughed and said, "Yeah, Mr. Jordan's really cool."

Sometimes it can be hard to approach a particular teacher. Like Carlos, you might need to ask another adult to speak to the teacher first or to be there when you talk to him or her. If you feel that the teacher is correcting you all of the time, you may get so angry that you start to blame the teacher for everything. It helps if you explain to the teacher or administrator how terrible it makes you feel to be singled out for criticism in the classroom. Ask them to talk to you in private, and say that you will do your best to change. Together the two of you can come up with some guidelines, like Carlos's list, to help you focus in class. Remember, if the first plan does not work, ask your teacher or counselor to help you change it. Don't be discouraged. Draw up some guidelines or signals to try until you get to the right choice for you.

Homework

Guidelines like the ones Carlos used can help if you don't know the assignment or get mixed up about it. But even when you are clear on the assignment, you still may not know where to start. It is easier to tackle your homework if you organize it first.

It is important to take the following three Giant Steps of Change: "OL & P."

Step 1: Organize Yourself

Step 2: Listen

Step 3: Proofread

Step 1. First of all, you have to find a way to organize yourself. Buy the most fantastic notebook you have ever seen. Copy the form into the front of the notebook. Use one form for each day of the school week. It is important to put your name on the top line. Write it with a sense of pride and ownership. This is yours.

Step 2. The second step is to listen carefully in class and write down the assignment. Once you let your mind wander off the subject in class, it is hard to start listening again. Ask your teacher to give you signals, such as touching you on the shoulder or pausing by your desk, to recall your attention at intervals. Try to train yourself to keep listening even if you find what the teacher is saying dull and boring. One way to improve your concentration skills is to write down the main words the teacher says. This is called taking notes. If you're taking notes, you have to concentrate. It's hard to write fast enough to catch everything, so don't worry about getting every word. Just get the most important ones. As your listening skills improve, you will miss less information and fewer assignments. Ask your teacher to see if you wrote the assignment down correctly, just to be sure.

Back to Step 1: organization. If it is a long assignment, break it down into sections that you can handle one by one. Write each section on your daily homework assignment report. Next write how long you think it will take you to do each section, as well as the time you need for the entire assignment.

Now play "Beat the Clock." Get all your homework supplies together in the best area you have to concentrate, away from distractions. You will need a timing device, such as a kitchen timer. Set the timer for the length of time you have estimated for the first section. See if you can finish before the timer rings.

As you finish each section, put the completed category on your form. This will give you a sense of accomplishment. Continue with each section until you finish the entire assignment.

Step 3. Finally, after you have completed the entire assignment, go back and proofread and double-check for errors. After you have corrected your mistakes, mark off the "proofread" line in your report form.

You will be surprised how rapidly you have completed the entire homework for the day. Strange as it may seem, breaking it into parts and using a timer will actually save you time.

With all of the negative experiences and only a few positive experiences associated with school, ADD/ADHD students often feel that school is a real drag. Can this be turned around? Yes! But only by you, the student. YOU must take control of your life. Ask for all the help you need, and then take charge of your own school experience.

Dealing with Your Family

Does your home sometimes feel like a battleground? The teen years can be troublesome in any family. For teens with ADD/ADHD, maintaining good relationships with parents and siblings may sometimes seem impossible. Research shows that ADD/ADHD tends to run in families. Children with ADD/ADHD usually have at least one close relative with the disorder. And more than 30 percent of all fathers who suffered from ADD/ADHD in their youth have children with ADD/ADHD. It makes it more difficult if you have a parent or sibling who also has ADD/ADHD. Like their children, parents with ADD/ADHD may be impulsive, impatient, and easily frustrated. This makes the situation at home harder for everyone.

Get Outside Help

If you and your family feel locked in a struggle, the best way to break out of it may be to go outside the family for help and a better perspective.

Whether they have ADD/ADHD themselves or not, encourage your parents to join a support group. Tell them that you know how hard it is for them to cope with your disorder and that talking to other parents of ADD/ADHD children may give them ideas and help them feel more optimistic that you can improve the situation. They may also find counseling or therapy helpful.

A support group and counseling or therapy can be a big help to you, too. Just finding out that you are not alone in your special problems is a big relief. You can also get some ideas on how to improve life at home.

If you have already been diagnosed with ADD/ADHD, you probably know that your parents will play an important role in helping you learn to manage the disorder. But perhaps you have a parent with a problem such as alcoholism or drug abuse. Or maybe your parents work so hard to pay the bills that they are just too exhausted to give you the help you need. If your parents are unavailable to you for any reason, it is all the more important that you find other adults to rely on for guidance and support with your ADD/ADHD. Make a list of adults you could consult for different kinds of help and support. Do you have a sympathetic relative, a school counselor, a teacher, a doctor, or a clergyperson you could talk to? You may even decide to ask them to talk to your parents for you.

To find an ADD/ADHD support group near you, call or write to one of the organizations listed in the Where to Go for Help section in this book and ask them for information. For help with alcoholism in the family, call the national number of Alcoholics Anonymous. There are groups to help with many kinds of family problems. You can also ask your school counselor or doctor where you can get help for your family.

Susan

Susan and her mother were very close, but they did have their moments. Sometimes they had major clashes. Susan's mother was a single parent who had been diagnosed with ADHD when she was in high school. Susan was diagnosed with ADHD when she was very young. Her pediatrician said she did not need medication. Susan and her mother both coped with their disorder by using behavior management techniques. But now that Susan was a teenager, it seemed as though she and her mother were fighting all the time. She was also having more difficulty with school and her friends. Her teachers suggested that she needed more help with her ADHD.

Susan and her mother decided to consult another doctor, Dr. Sullivan. The doctor said that she would like Susan to try Ritalin. She said she would ask Susan's teachers and mother to observe Susan carefully while she was trying the medication. She would need to adjust the dosage several times and try different medications to find the best one. Dr. Sullivan also arranged for Susan and her mother to go to therapy. They went to sessions together twice a month to work out their mutual problems. Susan went by herself the other two weeks of the month.

The therapist helped them discuss many of their feelings and conflicts. She gave them practical advice about how to resolve their disagreements instead of letting them get out of control. For instance, they agreed on a "zone out" instead of a "clash out." Whenever either of them felt tension rising, she had the option of calling "zone out" the way a referee calls "time out" in a ball game. Then they each went to a separate place. Later they discussed the situation when they were both calm and better able to focus. They also learned how to avoid getting into some arguments by using the techniques that follow.

Avoid Trip Phrases

You can start improving relations at home by seeing how the conflicts arise. For instance, how do your arguments start? Parents and children say certain things to each other that "trip their switches," making the other person angry. Before they know it, they are having another argument. Does this sound like you? Make up your own list and ask your parents to make one, too. Then, using the suggestions below for ideas, you and your parents can agree on some alternatives to try. Some "trip phrases" and possible alternative solutions include:

Teenager: "You never listen to me or pay attention to what I say!"

Alternative: "I need to talk to you. Is this a good time?"

(If it is not a good time, agree on a specific time later when you can talk.)

Teenager: "I'm not a criminal. Why do you treat me this way?"

Alternative: Agree in advance for your parent to allow

52

you to go to your room to calm down before discussing things when you are angry.

Teenager: "I get sick and tired of hearing you always say 'Think before you act' or 'Pay attention.'"

Alternative: Prearrange a hand signal or cue word. When you see the hand signal or hear the cue word, you know what it means without your parent's nagging you.

Parent: "There you go, lying about your homework again."

Alternative: Put a table by the front door for completed homework. The teen puts it there at a prearranged time for the parent to check. If it is not placed by the door in completed form by the agreed-upon time, the parent tapes a note on the teenager's door, "See you tomorrow at 4:00PM". This means the teenager is grounded the next evening after school. No verbal comments are needed. (It is critical that the teenager know where to get help with the homework. Teenager and parent need to discuss this with a school counselor or teacher. Look into tutors or other solutions if necessary.)

Parent: "Get up off your lazy duff and take the trash out. Why do I have to remind you of everything?"

Alternative: Put up a bulletin board listing chores for everyone in the family, including parents. Check off chores as they are completed. Set time limits, so everyone knows when things are to be done.

Respect Each Other

Parents want and expect the best for their children. A teenager may feel that he can never meet his parents' expectations. Or maybe he doesn't even want to be the kind of person his parents expect him to be. He may become angry and resentful. Many clashes may be ahead. ADD/ADHD children have more trouble than most children saying and doing the things their parents want them to say and do.

Parents should continue to want and to expect the best for their children, but they must also be in tune with their children. The parents' job is to discipline, structure, nurture, direct, and love. They must help their children be the best they can be for their own individual personality and talents.

Teenagers need to realize that the parents' job also includes helping their children develop a sense of responsibility, loyalty, respect, and love for themselves and others. Parents must be consistent in enforcing reasonable limits and structure. Because it is hard for ADD/ADHD children to accept structure, parents and children must work with special cooperation to create and accept the necessary rules.

As a teenager, you may look back on some mistakes your parents made with you and vow not to make the same mistakes with your children. Parents, too, realize mistakes that have been made in their lives. When they see their children starting to make the same mistakes, they may overreact and be too hard on their children. This makes the situation worse.

54

Shelly

"Young lady, you're not going anywhere with Brad until you finish your homework!" yelled Mrs. Wilkinson as she watched her daughter apply dark purple lipstick to her lips.

"Come on, Mom, you're not being fair!" whined Shelly. "You're such a witch! Can't you get off my back just for once?"

"Well, I'm not the one with an attention disorder!" fumed Mrs. Wilkinson. "I'm not the one who gets lousy grades and might never get into college!"

"You're just jealous because I'm going out with Brad and since Daddy left, you don't have anyone!" yelled Shelly.

With that, Shelly flounced out of the house, slamming the door behind her. Mrs. Wilkinson burst into tears and had to take an antidepressant pill.

Obviously, neither Shelly nor her mom knew how to deal with their frustration in a positive way. Because Shelly, who had ADHD, was distracted by thoughts of her boyfriend Brad, she wasn't able to concentrate on her homework. But instead of trying to negotiate with her mother—perhaps to go out with Brad for dinner only and then come home and complete all her assignments—she had defied her and hurt her. She knew her mother was only trying to help. Meanwhile, even if Mrs. Wilkinson sometimes found it tiring to deal with Shelly's ADHD, she never should have mentioned it the way she did. She knew that Shelly usually tried her best. Maybe Mrs.

Wilkinson was still hurting from having been abandoned by Shelly's dad and she was taking it out on Shelly.

The next day, both mother and daughter apologized to each other. They promised to always try to negotiate. If there was something Shelly wanted to do, they would agree in advance on how and if she could fit both work and play into her schedule. They also decided to do some joint counseling in order to deal with their obviously complicated feelings concerning Shelly's dad.

Charlie

Charlie was a special education student; he had a learning disability and he had ADHD. He needed to pay attention in class, but he couldn't concentrate. Charlie wished he could go home, but his dad was still drunk from the night before. Charlie had not been able to finish his homework because of his parents' fighting and his dad's drinking. He didn't know how to stop it. He had tried to intervene in the past, but both parents ended up yelling at him. He had seen his dad hit his mother more than once. What if his mother got hurt worse than bruises? He knew he would feel he should have stopped his dad. But how could he? Charlie felt angry and he was worried about his little brother and sister.

"Charlie, are you with us today?" the loud voice of Mr. Bradshaw, the English teacher, cut into his thoughts. "Do you have your homework?"

Charlie said, "I was not able to finish it."

Mr. Bradshaw said, "Charlie, please see Mr. Maxwell [the counselor] today."

After class, Charlie walked by Mr. Maxwell's office and hesitated at the door. Mr. Maxwell looked up and said, "Hello, Charlie. I've been wanting to talk to you. Can you come in for a few moments?"

Charlie told him Mr. Bradshaw had sent him. Mr. Maxwell said, "Several of your other teachers have also talked to me. You had been managing your ADHD so well since you started the medication and using the guidelines we worked out. But recently you seem to have a hard time concentrating. What is happening in your life?" Charlie remained silent. Mr. Maxwell continued. "Unless you tell me, I can't help you. My only alternative is to call your parents. Perhaps I should call your house now while you're here."

Charlie begged Mr. Maxwell not to call his house, muttering something about his dad being sick. He had never told anyone about his parents.

Mr. Maxwell continued, "I have wondered for some time whether your father might be having problems. If he is, the worst thing you can do is try to protect him. I understand the stress you are under, and I am here to help."

Charlie got very quiet. Then he started talking. As he talked, he felt a great relief. It was so good to be able to talk to someone who understood. After he finished telling his story, Mr. Maxwell said, "I will talk to your mother. She has to be part of this picture, too.

She will be mad at both of us at first. Later on, I think she'll be very proud of you for standing up and getting some help."

Mr. Maxwell was right. Charlie's mother was very angry and upset, but eventually she ended up getting counseling and going to Al-Anon. Charlie attended Alateen. These are groups that try to help people who have alcoholics in their families. His father continued drinking, but Charlie and his mother learned how to take care of themselves and the family.

Charlie completed the year without failing. It had been hard at first to discuss his father's problems with others, but Charlie was glad he had done it. Now he could think about his own life again instead of always worrying about his family.

Like Charlie, you may have major problems with your family that you cannot work out. Take the big step of asking for help from other adults in your life.

Family Basics

All parents and children have conflicts. If you have ADD/ADHD, you may feel that your family conflicts never stop. But with everyone's cooperation, you can reduce the level of tension in your home. Write down these basic guidelines and tape them up where you will see them often at home:

- ⮑ Identify and avoid your "trip phrases."

- ⮑ Separate and calm down before discussing an issue.

↪ Respect each other's roles and responsibilities in the family.

↪ Get outside help when needed.

Some organizations that can help are listed in the back of this book.

Dealing with Your Friends

Do you feel that your friends understand you? Do you understand them? These are big questions. Throughout your life, you will depend on your friends for many emotional and practical needs. And they will need to depend on you, too. Good friends are very important because they can really add to your happiness.

Most people have felt lonely and misunderstood at some point in their lives. It is perfectly normal for this kind of thing to happen. In fact, almost everyone grows apart from a friend or has disagreements at one time or another. If you have ADD/ADHD, you may actually find that these kinds of situations happen to you more often. You may have to work more carefully at making friends and at keeping them.

In the past, potential friends may have avoided you because you seemed too aggressive. Or, depending on your particular ADD/ADHD symptoms, people may have felt that you didn't listen to them or that you were too spaced out. Learning to use behavior management techniques, as we discussed in chapter 4, will help make you a better friend. For instance, knowing how to control your temper will prevent flare-ups and fights. A trained professional can help you with these important social skills. Medication may also be useful. Ask your doctor about this.

Who Are Your Friends?

While you work on improving your friendship skills, it would also be a good idea to figure out who your friends are now and whom you would like to have as friends. First, take stock of the friends you have. Copy the chart on page 62. Write down the names of the people who best match each category. Also list their relationship to you (include your friends, mother, father, sister, etc.). Next rate how well you meet each other's needs (good, fair, poor).

After you have filled out the chart, look at the first column to see if one or two names appear too frequently. If so, this is like putting all your eggs in one basket. If the basket gets dropped, you could have big problems. You may want to consider making some new friends.

Now read the second column. Are you relying too much on your family members? Or not enough?

Look at the third column to see if your friends are meeting your needs. Check the next column to see how well you rate yourself at meeting their needs. Is there room for improvement in some cases?

If you don't think you have been doing your part, think about how you could do better. If your friends are not meeting your needs in some areas, could they do more? Or should you think about making another friend? Remember, no one friend can meet all your needs. You might expect your best friend to understand a lot about

FRIENDSHIP CHART

	Names	Relationship	How well do they meet your needs?	How well do you meet their needs?
Who listens to you?				
Who gives you positive feedback by telling you what a fantastic person you are?				
Who provides challenges to help you do better in life?				
Who gives you emotional support when things do not go well?				
Who gives you spiritual support?				
Whom do you play or hang out with?				
Whom do you exercise with (bike, ride, run, play tennis or basketball, etc.)?				

you, and to talk to you about everything, including your ADD/ADHD. A more casual friend might be someone you just play games with. Some people are friends only at school or work.

Edward

Edward was feeling depressed. It was raining. He was bored and couldn't think of anything fun to do. He had tried to get a job, but he was only 15. Every place he tried said he had to be 16 before they would talk to him. He couldn't call any of his friends because they were fed up with him. They liked his energy, but they said he was too moody and temperamental and never listened to what they wanted to do. Edward blamed his ADHD for his moods. He knew he needed to do more work on the social skills he had learned from his counselor, but he didn't feel like it.

Edward turned on the television to see what was on. Just then the telephone rang, but it was for his sister June. He irritably called her to the telephone. When June got off the phone, she said her friend was coming by to take her to the mall. She asked Edward if he wanted to go with them. Edward jumped at the chance to do something, even if it was with his sister.

At the mall, June and her friend went shopping. They told Edward to meet them in two hours. Edward strolled around the mall, looking into the store windows. It was always difficult for him to stay in one place. Not watching what he was doing, he bumped into another teenager. The other boy frowned.

63

Edward felt himself getting angry, but instead he took a deep breath and apologized. He said, "You having a bad day, too?" The other boy said, "You better believe it. Nothing good has happened today." Edward said, "Me, too."

They began talking. Edward tried hard to listen and not to interrupt. Suddenly he remembered the time. He and his new friend had been talking for an hour. He had to rush to meet June. He and Philip exchanged telephone numbers and made plans to get together.

Edward was in a good mood now. He had done something positive for himself. He had been the first to speak and to be friendly.

ADHD teenagers can be good friends to others. Sometimes they need to work at it. To develop new friends, you have to find ways to meet people. You may have to go out of your way to be friendly first, like Edward. Your school counselor will be able to tell you about groups of teenagers that meet regularly. Choose a group with interests similar to your own. There may be clubs for science, music, art, or religion, for example.

You should also know how to avoid making friends with the wrong people. It may be tempting to be friends with someone just because they like you or seem to accept you the way you are. But listen to people first. Are they trustworthy? If they lie about themselves or others, or if they talk about people behind their backs, they will probably do the same to you. Do they use drugs? You must think carefully before getting involved with people who drink or use drugs. Most people give in to peer pressure, the pressure that they feel to join in whatever everyone else around them is doing. Drinking or using drugs is not a good idea for anyone. It is especially dangerous if you are already on medication, such as Ritalin, as many people with ADHD are. Drugs react when they are mixed together in someone's system. The reaction is never positive, and sometimes it can be fatal. Consider your choice of friends carefully.

When you make friends with someone, you are finding out what they are like on the inside. The only way to find out is to establish a line of communication with them. You have to be able to talk openly with them. That takes trust. The more you get to know them, the more openly you may talk and the more trust you may feel. Friends will be glad to find out what you are really like on the inside. Your ADD/ADHD need not be an obstacle to friendship.

Looking into the Future

Experts say that about two-thirds of ADD/ADHD cases persist into adulthood. However, some symptoms may change or decrease. Because you will be in different situations as an adult, your ADD/ADHD may affect you in different ways. For example, you will no longer have to go to school (unless you want to), so you won't have all those rules to follow and all those authority figures telling you what to do. On the other hand, you will have a job and a boss to answer to, and you will need to manage your ADD/ADHD so that you can be successful at work.

Adults who have never had their ADD/ADHD diagnosed may continue to have problems at home, at work, and with friends. And they may be more prone to depression and to drug and alcohol abuse. They are unaware of the cause of their behavior—ADD/ADHD—so they don't know how to change.

But if you are already trying to understand and manage your ADD/ADHD, you may cope even better as an adult, whether your symptoms seem to diminish or not as you grow older. You can be a happy, successful person.

You are investing in your future every time you improve your listening techniques, practice communicating with a friend, or even complete a homework assignment. You are creating a happier, more self-confident you by learning to manage your ADD/ADHD. The skills you are working on now—with school, friends, and family—are the skills you will need later for your job and your adult relationships. So your first preparation for a happy future is improving the present.

The next step is to dream about your future. People probably tell you that you dream too much. But we must do some dreaming about what we want so that we can plan how to achieve it. Copy the chart below. You can use it to start planning your future.

GOAL CHART

My current age ___
How old will I be in ten years? ___

My ten-year goals	Steps to take each year to reach my goals

Career goals
Relationship goals
Social goals
Spiritual goals

Career

Think of all the things you have ever imagined becoming. What dream career would you like to become a reality? Be sure to set your sights high enough. Many successful people have ADD/ADHD. It has been speculated that inventor and political leader Benjamin Franklin, British statesman Winston Churchill, scientist Albert Einstein, and perhaps even U.S. president Bill Clinton may have had attention deficit disorder (*Time*, July 18, 1994). Perhaps some of them even found ways to turn their disorder into an advantage by choosing careers in which their extra drive and energy were a big plus.

People with attention deficit disorders often do better in jobs that involve moving around physically. Some examples of jobs that can be more physically active are real estate or other sales jobs, restaurant work, jobs in the hotel/tourism industry, and some kinds of teaching and law. There are many other possibilities. Jobs that require a lot of paperwork and record keeping are usually more difficult choices.

Using your own goal chart, write down a ten-year career goal. Do you want to graduate from college? Do you want to graduate from a vocational-technical college? Do you want to work in a big corporation, a small business, a school, or in politics? Would you like to work with computers, plants, music, or people? If you were now what you dream of becoming, would you act differently? Would you walk or talk differently? If so, for the next week practice acting, walking, and talking as if you were whatever you chose for your ten-year career goal. See how it feels to be that special person you want to become. If you like the feeling, how can you make it happen?

ADD/ADHD can help you with extra energy, but you will have to devote extra work, commitment, and follow-through to make your dream become reality. Your school counselor can help you with career ideas. Fill in some ideas on your chart about what to accomplish each year to work toward your goal. What will you need to learn more about now? Science? Art? Health? Can you talk to adults you know about these jobs? What schools or colleges might you find out about?

Relationship and Social Goals

What do you dream of for your marriage or relationship goals in ten years? How will ADD/ADHD affect your relationships? The significant other person in your life will need to understand your disorder thoroughly. If you marry someone who thinks he or she can change you, chances are you will both be miserable. It would be a good idea for both you and your intended partner to talk to your family doctor or counselor before deciding to get married. Besides talking about your relationship with each other, you will need to discuss the fact that if you have children, there is a chance that they will have ADD/ADHD. How would you cope with this? Talking things through before marriage can really improve your future happiness.

What can you do now to become a better partner in the future? You may not even know the person now with whom you will spend the rest of your life. But if you can imagine the kind of person you will look for, you can imagine the kind of person they will want you to be.

You can start practicing in all your relationships now to be that person. Can you be a better listener? Better able to communicate how you are feeling? Better at taking time out when you are angry? Better able to channel your energy and enthusiasm in positive directions?

These are some of the areas to work on now for good relationships and social goals. To be mentally healthy, we all need to be close to a group of friends or relatives. Whether you are thinking about friendships or romance, you can start to create a happier future right now.

Spiritual Goals

The spiritual dimension of your life is also important. Developing your spiritual side can help you deal with despair, grief, or other strong feelings that most people encounter in their lives. A spiritual sense can give you a feeling of peace and fulfillment. It may seem strange to think of setting goals for spirituality. But if you lead a busy life, you may find you need to set aside some time specifically to let your spiritual thoughts and feelings develop. You may want to explore these through prayer, music, or worship in a religious group. You may prefer reflection or meditation, or spending time outdoors. Volunteering to help other people can also give you spiritual satisfaction. All of these can help you to feel part of something greater than just your own world.

Frank

Dr. Simpson's words were still ringing in Frank's ears as he left the office. Frank's mother was quiet, too, as she walked beside him.

Finally his mother spoke, "How do you feel about

Dr. Simpson's saying that your ADHD symptoms have improved so much?"

Frank thought, then answered, "I was surprised. But he is right. Things are easier. It has been a gradual change, I don't really know when it happened."

"I don't know when you changed either. But you are definitely different than when you were in elementary school and junior high school," his mother replied.

Frank was completing his first year of training at a vocational-technical school. He was making average or above-average grades. He was happy with himself and had made friends with some of his classmates. Frank had qualified for a scholarship, and the school had helped him get a part-time job. He was pleased to be putting himself through school because his parents didn't have the money to help him. One more year and Frank would be out on his own with a full-time job. He was looking forward to that time.

Emerson

"Daddy," said eight-year-old Corinne as her dad helped her put the finishing touches on her water-color painting. "When I grow up I think I want to be just like you."

Emerson looked up and exchanged happy glances with his wife, Sue-Ellen.

"It's true, hon," said Sue-Ellen, giving Emerson a big hug. "I've never seen you as calm and patient as you are with little Corinne."

Emerson felt great. Who would have thought that someday someone would be describing him as "calm and patient"? Emerson remembered when he was just a little older than Corinne was—he was the least calm and patient person possible. He was always getting into fights and trouble. He had no friends and had already been held back twice in school. His parents thought he was slow. His teachers thought he was out of control. His friends...well, come to think of it he didn't have any friends back then. By the age of twelve, he was already convinced that he was a brain-dead, good-for-nothing boy who would never amount to anything.

When he was thirteen, he got kicked out of school and was sent to a school for "problem" children. Only, as a counselor at the school discovered, Emerson wasn't a "problem" child. The only "problem" with Emerson was that nobody had caught on to the fact that he had ADHD.

Once he and his parents became aware of the disorder, they did everything they could to deal with it. It really helped that they finally knew what they were up against. With the help of his parents and teachers, with therapy and medication, and with lots of hard work and determination, Emerson tried to live life to the best of his potential. And by the time he graduated from high school—in the top 20 percent of his class—he found that he had not only tried, but he had succeeded.

Although Emerson had always had some trouble with his more academic subjects, he discovered that he really loved art, particularly painting. After graduating, he went to art college. There, he not only perfected his own painting, but he took courses in art education. When he finished the program, he was immediately hired to teach art to kids with learning disabilities. Some of the kids in his class even had ADD and ADHD. The principal who hired him, Ms. Ramirez, was not only impressed with Emerson's art, but with his teaching skills, his compassion, and the way he related to kids. "You're a great example to these children," she said after observing one of his classes. "Those kids really look up to you as someone who has made it despite his disabilities."

Teaching helped Emerson feel good about himself. It also paid the bills while he pursued his own painting. During his first exhibition, he met and fell in love with Sue-Ellen, the owner of a small art gallery. Within a year they were married. Although Emerson worried about having a child with Sue-Ellen—he was afraid a child of his might have ADD or ADHD, and he didn't want to see a child of his suffer the way he had—Sue-Ellen said he was silly. "Just look at what a success you turned out to be. The fact that you had ADHD didn't stop you at all," she pointed out.

Feeling Good

Teenagers often feel that they are branded or stamped for life because they have ADD/ADHD. They may feel they have no future because they are convinced they are dumb or stupid. They may have very low self-esteem.

You are not stupid, or lazy, or bad, or whatever else people may have said to you over the years. If you have ADD/ADHD, you have a disability. And disabilities can be overcome. We can each determine our own destiny. We can even find positive elements in ADD/ADHD. The real disability is attitude.

The Real Disability Is Attitude

One of the best predictors of success in coping with

Weakness Becomes Strength
Impatience /Impulsiveness Becomes Energy, Activeness
Moodiness Becomes Creativity
Easy Boredom Becomes Enthusiasm
Difficulty with Rules and Authority Becomes Problem-Solving and Taking Control
Trouble Switching Mental Gears Becomes Super-Focus

ADD/ADHD may be your attitude. Let's see how you can improve your attitude by changing negatives into positives. Coping with ADD/ADHD doesn't mean only managing the disorder. It also means adapting to it and building on your strengths.

Impatience and Impulsiveness

If people say you are impatient and impulsive, realize that they may be right. Rephrase it mentally; the positive side is that you are active and energetic. Think of yourself as an expensive, finely tooled Ferrari racing car. You have an accelerator, but you must also have brakes or you will crash. It is all right for you to go fast at times, just as it is all right for the Ferrari to go fast in appropriate places. If it goes at 100 miles per hour on a racetrack, everyone cheers. If it goes 100 miles per hour though a school zone, it could crash and hurt people. The key is "appropriate place." For example, it is not appropriate for you to tell your teacher to "stuff it" in the middle of a classroom full of students. But it is appropriate for you to tell your teacher to "stuff it" while you are doing homework at home. You will be cheered if you run fast when competing on your school's track team, but you could be in trouble if you run at the same speed through the halls at school. It is often not what we do but where we choose to do it that causes our difficulties.

Notice the word choose. You are in control of your life, and you make the decision whether to put on your brakes or go full speed. Anything that runs out of control is dangerous.

One technique some ADD/ADHD teenagers find help-ful is to visualize an imaginary speed control knob inside themselves. When it is turned to "high" or "fast," they experience everything in extremes. They get extremely impatient or impulsive, extremely upset or angry. Some things need to be done fast. ADHD teens are experts at speed.

They can also learn to turn the control knob to a slow speed when appropriate. Visualize a knob inside you. Is it in your brain? Is it in your finger? Is it in your chest? When you are in a "go slow" situation, turn your imaginary speed control down to "slow." Now you can go at the appropriate pace.

Moodiness

If you are moody, can you figure out what causes your moodiness? Suppose a guy named James came up to you and called you stupid, then walked off. You would prob-ably feel upset. If Sue then walked up and said, "Hi," you might respond angrily to her. She would think you were moody.

Since you are in control of your life, instead of being moody with Sue you could become creative. Think ahead of time of something funny to say to James the next time he calls you stupid. What would James do if you respond-ed by laughing and saying, "Well, at least I'm not rude like some people I know," and then you walked off.

Then when you met Sue you would probably still be laughing, thinking of James feeling like a jerk. When Sue said, "Hi," you would be in a great mood.

Boredom

If you are easily bored, figure out what bores you. Take control of those things, and you may be able to change your attitude from boredom to enthusiasm.

For instance, you may have five pages of math home-work problems to do when you want to be out with your friends. You know how to do math. The problems just take so long! You think it is stupid to spend so much time on something you know how to do. Take control of the situation and find a time and creative way to do them.

For example, you might divide the task into smaller units. Fold each page in half or even fourths. Set a kitchen timer and try to "beat the clock" by finishing each section before it rings. You may save so much time that you are able to join your friends for part of the evening.

If not, have another reward waiting for you when you finish. Play your favorite music or computer game if you finish before the timer goes off three out of four times. Since you are in control, you set your own reward.

Rules

If you have difficulty with rules and authority, try to figure out what particularly bothers you about the rule or being told what to do. Then look for a way to make the rule more acceptable. If your mother is standing in the living room looking at the clock each night when you come in, it may not be the rule that bothers you. It may be the fact that your mother is checking on you. Use your creativity and come up with another solution. Maybe she could go to bed and you could come in and wake her up when you get home. If your mother is afraid that something might happen to you and that she won't know about it, she could set her alarm clock.

When you come in and awaken her, she can turn it off. If you do not show by the appointed hour, the alarm will go off and she will be aware there is a problem. Again, you're in control.

Switching Gears

Do you have trouble switching gears or do you get upset easily when you are interrupted? Try thinking of yourself as someone who is a superfocused person. ADD/ADHD students are frequently accused of not paying attention. Instead, they may be superfocused on something else. Use your creativity and find a way to turn this ability to be extremely focused into an asset. Being superfocused can help you get one job done at a time.

Take control of the situation and figure out a cue to help you direct your "superfocus" where it needs to be. If you need to change your focus in class, for example, you might ask your teacher to walk over and lightly touch you on the shoulder when she notices you are not listening to her. You've come up with a method to keep your focus.

Darnell

Ellen thought Darnell was one of the most handsome

and popular boys in school. He was a track star. She knew Darnell had ADHD. He had confided to her that he used an imaginary inner control knob to cope with his ADHD. He needed to turn himself up for maximum speed at track, or when he got depressed. He touched his right ear to turn up his inner control knob. He touched his left ear to help himself slow down if he felt angry or impatient when it was inappropriate to show it. Darnell also turned the imaginary knob to help him relax and slow down to go to sleep at night.

Ellen had seen Darnell put his finger on his ear at times but thought nothing of it. Now she thought his creativity was one of the reasons he was so popular. He had ADHD, but he was always coming up with interesting ways to keep a positive attitude about it. Ellen thought Darnell was fantastic for coping so well.

Suki

Remember Suki from chapter I? People weren't yelling at her as much anymore. In the year since she had been diagnosed with ADD, life had improved Suki.

First her doctor had tried several medications for her. After a short time they had found the right medication at the minimum dosage she needed. Her symptoms seemed more manageable right away.

Then Suki had started a program with a therapist to

learn behavior management and other coping skills. Her parents had also gone to the therapist, and they used their new techniques at home. Together they helped Suki work out an education plan with her teachers. She was finishing her homework now, and her grades have gone up.

The best thing was how Suki felt about herself. She had more self-confidence and she was happier. She has ADD, but she knew she could cope with it. With the help and support of people who cared about her, Suki felt that he could finally take charge of her life.

Glossary

Al-Anon Organization formed for spouses, family members, and friends of alcoholics.

Alateen Organization formed for children of alcoholics. It arose from Alcoholics Anonymous.

attention deficit disorder (ADD) Neurobiological disorder marked by habitual inability to pay attention for more than a few minutes, even when requested or punished.

attention deficit hyperactivity disorder (ADHD) attention deficit disorder accompanied by extreme overactivity.

deficit Lack or impairment of a capacity to function.

genetic Of or relating to a gene, the building block of heredity.

hereditary Transmitted from parent to offspring.

hyperactivity Excessive motor functioning or activity.

IEP (individualized education plan) Comprehensive written plan for special education and all related services.

impulsivity Form of impulsive behavior in which a person acts without logically thinking through the action or situation.

multimodal Treatment of a disorder by several methods at the same time.

neurobiological Concerned with the anatomy, physiology, and pathology of the nervous system.

perception Process by which the central nervous system organizes sensory information it receives.

psychologist Person holding an advanced degree (Ph.D.) in the study of the mental or behavioral characteristics of a person or group.

Tourette's syndrome Neurological disorder characterized by involuntary behavior such as multiple neck jerks and vocal grunts, barks, and sometimes obscenities. It is named for the French neurologist Georges Gille de la Tourette, who described it in 1885.

Appendix
Medical Management of Children with Attention Deficit Disorder: Commonly Asked Questions

By
Children with Attention Deficit Disorder (CH.A.D.D.)
American Academy of Child and Adolescent Psychiatry
(AACAP)
Committee of Community Psychiatry and Consultation to
Agencies of AACAP

Harvey C. Parker, Ph.D.
CH.A.D.D., Executive Director
George Storm, M.D.
CH.A.D.D., Professional Advisory Board
Theodore A. Petti, M.D., M.P.H., Chairperson
Virginia Q. Anthony, AACAP, Executive Director

This article may be reproduced and distributed
without written permission.

1. What Is an Attention Deficit Disorder?

Attention deficit disorder (ADD), also known as attention deficit hyperactivity disorder (ADHD), is a treatable disorder which affects approximately three to five percent of the population. Inattentiveness, impulsivity, and oftentimes, hyperactivity, are common characteristics of the disorder. Boys with ADD tend to outnumber girls by three to one, although ADD in girls is under-identified.

Some common symptoms of ADD are:

1. Excessively fidgets or squirms

2. Difficulty remaining seated

3. Easily distracted

4. Difficulty awaiting turn in games

5. Blurts out answers to questions

6. Difficulty following instructions

7. Difficulty sustaining attention

8. Shifts from one activity to another

9. Difficulty playing quietly

10. Often talks excessively

11. Often interrupts

12. Often doesn't listen to what is said

13. Often loses things

14. Often engages in dangerous activities

However, you don't have to be hyperactive to have an attention deficit disorder. In fact, up to 30 percent of children with ADD are not hyperactive at all, but still have a lot of trouble focusing their attention.

2. How Can We Tell If a Child Has ADD?

Many factors can cause children to have problems paying attention besides an attention deficit disorder. Family problems, stress, discouragement, drugs, physical illness, and learning difficulties can all cause problems that look like ADD, but really aren't. To accurately identify whether a child has ADD, a comprehensive evaluation needs to be performed by professionals who are familiar with characteristics of the disorder.

STRESS
DISCOURAGEMENT
PHYSICAL ILLNESS
LEARNING DIFFICULTIES
FAMILY PROBLEMS

The process of evaluating whether a child has ADD usually involves a variety of professionals, which can include the family physician, pediatrician, child and adolescent psychiatrist or psychologist, neurologist, family counselor and teacher. Psychiatric interview, psychological and educational testing, and/or a neurological examination can provide information leading to a proper diagnosis and treatment plan. An accurate evaluation is necessary before proper treatment can begin. Complex cases in which the diagnosis is unclear or is complicated by other medical and psychiatric conditions should be seen by a physician.

Parents and teachers, being the primary sources of information about the child's ability to attend and focus at home and in school, play an integral part in the evaluation process.

3. What Kinds of Services and Programs Help Children with ADD and Their Families?

Help for the ADD child and the family is best provided through multimodal treatment delivered by a team of professionals who look after the medical, emotional, behavioral, and educational needs of the child. Parents play an essential role as coordinators of services and programs designed to help their child. Such services and programs may include:

- Medication to help improve attention and reduce impulsivity and hyperactivity, as well as to treat other emotional or adjustment problems which sometimes accompany ADD.

- Training parents to understand ADD and to be more effective behavior managers as well as advocates for their child.

- Counseling or training ADD children in methods

of self-control, attention focusing, learning strategies, organizational skills, or social skill development.

⮑ Psychotherapy to help the demoralized or even depressed ADD child.

⮑ Other interventions at home and at school designed to enhance self-esteem and foster acceptance, approval, and a sense of belonging.

4. What Medications Are Prescribed for ADD Children?

Medications can dramatically improve attention span and reduce hyperactive and impulsive behavior. Psychostimulants have been used to treat attentional deficits in children since the 1940s. Antidepressants, while used less frequently to treat ADD, have been shown to be quite effective for the management of this disorder in some children.

5. How Do Psychostimulants such as Dexedrine (dextroamphetamine), Ritalin (methylphenidate) and Cylert (pemoline) Help?

Seventy to eighty percent of ADD children respond in a positive manner to psychostimulant medication. Exactly how these medicines work is not known. However, benefits for children can be quite significant and are most apparent when concentration is required. In classroom settings, on-task behavior and completion of assigned tasks is increased, socialization with peers and teacher is improved, and disruptive behaviors (talking out, demanding attention, getting out of seat, noncompliance with requests, breaking rules) are reduced.

The specific dose of medicine must be determined for each child. Generally, the higher the dose, the greater the effect and side effects. To ensure proper dosage, regular monitoring at different levels should be done. Since there are no clear guidelines as to how long a child should take medication, periodic trials off medication should be done to determine continued need. Behavioral rating scales, testing on continuous performance tasks, and the child's self-reports provide helpful, but not infallible measures of progress.

Despite myths to the contrary, a positive response to stimulants is often found in adolescents with ADD; therefore, medication need not be discontinued as the child reaches adolescence if it is still needed.

6. What Are Common Side Effects of Psychostimulant Medications?

Reduction in appetite, loss of weight, and problems in falling asleep are the most common adverse effects. Children treated with stimulants may become irritable and more sensitive to criticism or rejection. Sadness and a tendency to cry are occasionally seen.

The unmasking or worsening of a tic disorder is an infrequent effect of stimulants. In some cases this involves Tourette's syndrome. Generally, except in Tourette's, the tics decrease or disappear with the discontinuation of the stimulant. Caution must be employed in medicating adolescents with stimulants if there are coexisting disorders, e.g., depression, substance abuse, conduct, tic or mood disorders. Likewise, caution should be employed when a family history of a tic disorder exists.

Some side effects, e.g., decreased spontaneity, are felt to be dose-related and can be alleviated by reduction of dosage or switching to another stimulant. Similarly, slowing of height and weight gain of children on stimulants has been documented, with a return to normal for both occurring upon discontinuation of the medication. Other less common side effects have been described but they may occur as frequently with a placebo as with active medication. Pemoline may cause impaired liver functioning in 3 percent of children, and this may not be completely reversed when this medication is discontinued.

Overmedication has been reported to cause impairment in cognitive functioning and alertness. Some children on higher doses of stimulants will experience what has been described as a "rebound" effect, consisting of changes in mood, irritability and increases of the symptoms associated with their disorder. This occurs with variable degrees of severity during the late afternoon or evening, when the level of medicine in the blood falls. Thus, an additional low dose of medicine in the late afternoon or a decrease of the noontime dose might be required.

7. When Are Tricyclic Antidepressants Such as Tofranil (imipramine), Norpramin (desipramine) and Elavil (amytriptyline) Used to Treat ADD Children?

This group of medications is generally considered when

contraindications to stimulants exist, when stimulants have not been effective or have resulted in unacceptable side effects, or when the antidepressant property is more critical to treatment than the decrease of inattentiveness. They are used much less frequently than the stimulants, seem to have a different mechanism of action, and may be somewhat less effective than the psychostimulants in treating ADD. Long-term use of the tricyclics has not been well studied. Children with ADD who are also experiencing anxiety or depression may do best with an initial trial of a tricyclic antidepressant followed with a stimulant for the more classic ADD Symptoms (if needed).

8. What Are the Side Effects of Tricyclic Antidepressant Medications?

Side effects include constipation and dry mouth. Symptomatic treatment with stool softeners and sugar free gum or candy are usually effective in alleviating the discomfort. Confusion, elevated blood pressure, possible precipitation of manic-like behavior and inducement of seizures are uncommon side effects. The latter three occur in vulnerable individuals who can generally be identified during the assessment phase.

9. What About ADD Children Who Do Not Respond Well to Medication?

Some ADD children or adolescents will not respond satisfactorily to either the psychostimulant or tricyclic antidepressant medications. Non-responders may have severe symptoms of ADD, may have other problems in addition to ADD, or may not be able to tolerate certain medications due to adverse side effects as noted above. In such cases consultation with a child and adolescent psychiatrist may be helpful.

10. How Often Should Medications Be Dispensed at School to an ADD Child?

Since the duration for effective action for Ritalin and Dexedrine, the most commonly used psychostimulants, is only about four hours, a second dose during school is often required. Taking a second dose of medication at noontime enables the ADD child to focus attention effectively, utilize appropriate school behavior and maintain academic productivity. However, the noon-time dose can sometimes be eliminated for children whose afternoon academic schedule does not require high levels of attentiveness. Some psychostimulants, i.e., SR Ritalin (sustained release form) and Cylert, work for longer periods of time (eight to ten hours) and may help avoid the need for a noontime dose. Antidepressant medications used to treat ADD are usually taken in the morning, afternoon hours after school, or in the evening.

In many cases the physician may recommend that medication be continued at non-school times such as weekday afternoons, weekends, or school vacations. During such non-school times, lower doses of medication than those taken for school may be sufficient. It is important to remember that ADD is more than a school problem—it is a problem which often interferes in the learning of constructive social, peer, and sports activities.

11. How Should Medication Be Dispensed at School?

Most important, regardless of who dispenses medication, since an ADD child may already feel "different" from others, care should be taken to provide discreet reminders to the child when it is time to take medication. It is quite important that school personnel treat the administration of medication in a sensitive manner, thereby safeguarding the privacy of the child or adolescent and avoiding any unnecessary embarrassment. Success in doing this will increase the student's compliance in taking medication.

The location for dispensing medication at school may vary depending upon the school's resources. In those schools with a full-time nurse, the infirmary would be the first choice. In those schools in which a nurse is not always available, other properly trained school personnel may take the responsibility of supervising and dispensing medication.

12. How Should the Effectiveness of Medication and Other Treatments for the ADD Child Be Monitored?

Important information needed to judge the effectiveness of medication usually comes from reports by the child's parents and teachers and should include information about the child's behavior and attentiveness, academic performance, social and emotional adjustment, and any medication side effects.

Reporting from these sources may be informal through telephone, or more objective via the completion of scales designed for this purpose.

The commonly used teacher rating scales are:

➥ Conners Teacher Rating Scales

➥ ADD-H Comprehensive Teacher Rating Scale

➥ Child Behavior Checklist

➥ ADHD Rating Scale

➥ Child Attention Problems (CAP) Rating Scale

➥ School Situations Questionnaire

Academic performance should be monitored by comparing classroom grades prior to and after treatment.

It is important to monitor changes in peer relationships, family functioning, social skills, a capacity to enjoy leisure time, and self-esteem.

The parents, school nurse, or other school personnel responsible for dispensing or overseeing the medication trial should have regular contact by phone with the prescribing physician. Physician office visits of sufficient frequency to monitor treatment are critical in the overall care of children with ADD.

13. What Is the Role of the Teacher in the Care of Children with ADD?

Teaching an ADD child can test the limits of any educator's time and patience. As any parent of an ADD child will tell you, being on the front lines helping these children to manage on a daily basis can be both challenging and exhausting. It helps if teachers know what to expect and if they receive in-service training on how to teach and manage ADD students in their classrooms.

Here are some ideas that teachers told us have helped:

- Build upon the child's strengths by offering a great deal of encouragement and praise for the child's efforts, no matter how small.

- Learn to use behavior modification programs that motivate students to focus attention, behave better, and complete work.

- Talk with the child's parents and find helpful strategies that have worked with the child in the past.

- If the child is taking medication, communicate frequently with the physician (and parents) so that proper adjustments can be made with respect to type or dose of medication. Behavior rating scales are good for this purpose.

- Modify the classroom structure to accommodate the child's span of attention, i.e., shorter assignments, preferential seating in the classroom,

appealing curriculum material, animated presenta-
tion of lessons, and frequent positive reinforcement.

➪ Determine whether the child can be helped
through special educational resources within the
school.

➪ Consult with other school personnel such as the
guidance counselor, school psychologist, or
school nurse to get their ideas as well.

14. What Are Common Myths Associated with ADD Medications?

Myth: Medication should be stopped when a child
reaches teen years.

Fact: Research clearly shows that there is continued
benefit to medication for those teens who meet criteria
for diagnosis of ADD.

Myth: Children build up a tolerance of medication.

Fact: Although the dose of medication may need
adjusting from time to time, there is no evidence that
children build up a tolerance to medication.

Myth: Taking medication for ADD leads to greater
likelihood of later drug addiction.

Fact: There is no evidence to indicate that ADD medication leads to an increased likelihood of later drug
addiction.

Myth: Positive response to medication is confirmation
of a diagnosis of ADD.

Fact: The fact that a child shows improvement of
attention span or a reduction of activity while taking

ADD medication does not substantiate the diagnosis of ADD. Even some normal children will show a marked improvement in attentiveness when they take ADD medications.

Myth: Medication stunts growth.

Fact: ADD medications may cause an initial and mild slowing of growth, but over time the growth suppression effect is minimal if non-existent in most cases.

Myth: Taking ADD medications as a child makes you more reliant on drugs as an adult.

Fact: There is no evidence of increased medication taking when medicated ADD children become adults, nor is there evidence that ADD children become addicted to their medications.

Myth: ADD children who take medication attribute their success only to medication.

Fact: When self-esteem is encouraged, a child taking medication attributes his success not only to the medication but to himself as well.

Summary of Important Points

1. ADD children make up 3-5% of the population. but many children who have trouble paying attention may have problems other than ADD. A thorough evaluation can help determine whether attentional deficits are due to ADD or to other conditions.

2. Once identified, children with ADD are best treated with a multimodal approach. The best results

occur when behavioral management programs, educational interventions, parent training, counseling, and medication, when needed, are used together to help the ADD child. Parents of children and adolescents with ADD play the key role of coordinating these services.

3. Each ADD child responds in his or her own unique way to medication depending upon the child's physical make-up, severity of ADD symptoms, and other possible problems accompanying the ADD. Responses to medication need to be monitored and reported to the child's physician.

4. Teachers play an essential role in helping the ADD child feel comfortable within the classroom procedures, and work demands, sensitivity to self-esteem issues, and frequent parent-teacher contact can help a great deal.

5. ADD may be a lifelong disorder requiring lifelong assistance. Families, and the children themselves, need our continued support and understanding.

6. Successful treatment of the medical aspects of ADD is dependent upon ongoing collaboration between the prescribing physician, teacher, therapist, and parents.

Where to Go for Help

In the United States

A.D.D. WareHouse
300 Northwest 70th Avenue, Suite 102
Plantation, FL 33317
(800) 233-9273
http://www.addwarehouse.com/

Children with Attention Deficit/Hyperactivity
    Disorder (CH.A.D.D.)
8181 Professional Place, Suite 201
Landover, MD 20785
(800) 233-4050
http://www.chadd.org/

Learning Disabilities Association
4156 Library Road
Pittsburgh, PA 15234
(412) 341-1515
http://www.ldanatl.org/

National Attention Deficit Disorder Association (NADD)
1788 Second Street, Suite 200
Highland Park, IL 60035
(847) 432-2332
http://www.add.org/

National Center for Learning Disabilities
381 Park Avenue South, Suite 1401
New York, NY 10016
1-888-575-7373
http://ncld.org/

National Information Center for Children and Youth
    with Disabilities (NICHCY)
P.O. Box 1492
Washington, DC 20013
(800) 695-0285
http://www.nichcy.org/

In Canada

Integra – (for Children and Adolescents with
    Learning Disabilities)
25 Imperial Street
Toronto, ON M5P 1B9
(416) 486-8055
http://home.iSTAR.ca/~integra/

Learning Disabilities Association of Canada
323 Chapel Street
Ottawa, ON K1N 7Z2
(613) 238-5721
http://edu-ss10.educ.queensu.ca/~lda/

Web Sites:

ADDitude - the lifestyle magazine for people with ADD
http://www.additudemag.com/

The ADDMed HomePage – by Dr. Anthony R. Laws, M.D.
http://www.addmed.com/

ADDvance - Magazine Resource Site for Women and
    Girls with Attention Deficit Disorder
http://www.addvance.com/

Mining Company Guide to ADD
http://add.miningco.com/

UnnaWhim with ADD
http://members.aol.com/UnnaWhim/index.html

For Further Reading

Beal, Eileen. *Everything You Need to Know About ADD/ADHD*. New York: Rosen Publishing Group, 1998.

Crist, James. *ADHD: A Teenager's Guide*. King of Prussia, PA: Center For Applied Psychology, 1996.

Cummings, R., and G. Fisher. *The Survival Guide for Teenagers with LD*. Minneapolis: Free Spirit, 1993.

Fellman, W. R. *The Other Me: Poetic Thoughts on ADD for Adults, Kids, and Parents*. Plantation, FL: Specialty Press, 1997.

Fenwick, Elizabeth, and Richard Walker. *Adolescence: The Survival Guide for Parents and Teenagers*. Dorling Kindersley Publishing, 1995.

Hartman, Thom. *Think Fast! The ADD Experience*. Grass Valley, CA: Underwood Books, 1995.

Levine, Mel. *Keeping a Head in School: A Student's Book About Learning Abilities and Learning Disorders*. Cambridge: Educators Publishing Service, 1994.

Nadeau, Kathleen. *Help4ADD@Highschool*. Bethesda, MD: Advantage Press, 1998.

Quinn, Patricia. *Adolescents and ADD: Gaining the Advantage*. New York: Magination Press, 1995.

Weiss, Lynn. *Give Your ADD Teen a Chance: A Guide for Parents of Teenagers with Attention Deficit Disorder*. Colorado Springs, CO: Pinon Press, 1996.

Index

communication, 65, 66, 69
concentration, 7, 14, 15,
    25, 38, 44, 47, 55,
    56, 57
consequences, weighing, 4
counseling/therapy, 16, 25,
    26, 28, 30-31, 32,
    50, 51, 56
    for parents, 31, 49-50,
    80
Cylert, 23

D

depression, 2, 7, 8, 24, 30,
    63, 66, 79
desipramine, 24
Dexedrine, 23
dextroamphetamine, 23
Diagnostic and Statistical
    Manual of Mental
    Disorders, 8, 9
distractibility, 1, 3, 4, 10,
    14, 34
drug use/abuse, 50, 65, 66

E

education/school plan, 15,
    16, 28, 29-30, 39,
    80
EEG biofeedback, 26
Einstein, Albert, 68
expectations, parental, 54

F

fidgeting, 7, 10, 13, 14,
    15, 34

fine-motor tests, 11, 13
focusing, 2, 3, 7, 35, 46, 78
forgetfulness, 1, 10, 24, 29,
    32
Franklin, Benjamin, 68
friends
    making new, 63-65
    taking stock of, 61-63
friendship chart, 62
frustration, 26, 49, 55

G

Giant Steps of Change, 46-
    48
goal chart, 67
goals
    career, 67-69
    relationship and social,
    69-70
    spiritual, 70
Goldstein, Sam, 3
guidelines, classroom, 44-
    46, 57
guidelines, family, 58-59

H

handwriting, 13
hearing problems, 8
heredity, 6, 49
homework, 46-48, 77
    completing, 2, 26, 29,
    32, 33, 48, 56, 66,
    80
    proofreading, 46, 48
homework assignment
    chart, 45